About the Author™

Meet
Gail Carson Levine

Alice B. McGinty

The Rosen Publishing Group's
PowerKids Press™
New York

To Gail

Published in 2003 by The Rosen Publishing Group, Inc.
29 East 21st Street, New York, NY 10010

First Edition

Editor: Frances E. Ruffin
Book Design: Maria E. Melendez

Photo Credits: All photos courtesy of Gail Carson Levine except p. 19, by Maura B. McConnell.

Grateful acknowledgment is made for permission to reprint previously published material: p. 13 (sidebar): Used by permission of HarperCollins Publishers.

McGinty, Alice B.
    Meet Gail Carson Levine / Alice B. McGinty.— 1st ed.
        p. cm. — (About the author)
    Summary: Presents a brief biography of the American author who wrote the 1998 Newbery Honor award-winning book "Ella Enchanted" while commuting from her home in Brewster, New York, to her job in New York City.
    Includes bibliographical references and index.
    ISBN 0-8239-6409-4
    1. Levine, Gail Carson—Juvenile literature. 2. Authors, American—20th century—Biography—Juvenile literature.
    3. Children's stories—Authorship—Juvenile literature. [1. Levine, Gail Carson. 2. Authors, American. 3. Authorship.
    4. Women—Biography.] I. Title. II Series.
    PS3562.E8965 Z77 2003
    813'.54—dc1

                                    2002000110

Manufactured in the United States of America

Contents

gail carson levine

On the Metro-North

Nobody noticed the small woman on the Metro-North train that traveled from New York City to the village of Brewster. That was fine with her. The woman, Gail Carson Levine, had a whole kingdom to worry about. With her fountain pen flying, and words spinning onto paper, Gail was writing a story. She liked nothing better than a **character** with spirit. Like the characters in her stories, Gail has spirit. As a child, she had climbed the steep rocks of the Palisades on the New York side of the Hudson River. She called them danger rocks. She had **rebelled** as a teenager. As an adult, she had the spirit to keep trying for nine long years to get her stories **published**.

Gail posed for this photo for her graduation from George Washington High School in 1964.

Gail Carson Levine wrote the story Ella Enchanted *while she rode the Metro-North train to and from her job in New York City.*

A Creative Family

Gail Ann Carson was born on September 17, 1947, in New York City. She was born into a creative family. Gail's mother, Sylvia, was a teacher. She wrote plays for her classes to perform. Gail's father, David, was a joyful man who owned a **commercial** art studio. David and Sylvia encouraged Gail and Gail's older sister, Rani, to be creative. Rani, who was five and a half years older than Gail, enjoyed painting. Rani grew up to become a fine arts professor and a painter of scenes and people from the island of **Jamaica**. Young Gail enjoyed painting, drawing pictures, practicing lines from plays, and saying tongue twisters. Gail also loved books. Fairy tales were among her favorites.

When Gail was young, her parents read to her. In first grade, Gail learned to read herself. From then on, she read and read! Gail's favorite books as a child included Anne of Green Gables *and* Peter Pan.

Gail starred in a high school play (left). *Gail and her older sister, Rani, dressed up* (right). ▶

School and Scribble Scrabble

Gail was a bright student at P.S. 173, her elementary school in the New York City neighborhood of Washington Heights. She and some friends formed a writing club, which they called the Scribble Scrabble Club. In the fifth grade, Gail played one of the two characters in a class play. She learned her lines immediately, so she didn't feel that she needed to **rehearse**. Sadly, when the play opened in front of the whole school, Gail forgot all of her lines. That didn't stop her from acting again, though. In high school, Gail successfully played the lead in a school play. She formed a theater group that performed for older people who lived in nursing homes.

◀ *Gail (circled) posed with her fifth-grade class at P.S. 173.*

Reading books helped Gail to find privacy in her family's small apartment. Gail shared a bedroom with her older sister. Books helped Gail escape to her own world. Sometimes she spent hours reading in the family's only bathroom!

Working Life

After graduating from high school in New York City, Gail entered Antioch College in Ohio. She finished her studies at City College of the City University of New York. She studied **philosophy** and graduated in 1969, with a Bachelor of Arts degree. While she was at Antioch, Gail met David Levine. One evening, when David lit a match, his bushy hair caught on fire. He didn't notice the fire until he saw the shocked look on Gail's face. Despite that event, Gail and David married in September 1967. Gail worked for the New York state government, helping **unemployed** people to find jobs. She enjoyed being able to help people.

Years ago, Gail and David wrote a children's musical. David wrote the songs, and Gail wrote the script, or the story. They were excited when their musical, Spacenapped, was produced by a neighborhood theater in Brooklyn, New York.

Gail had fun with her husband, David, and a snowy friend during college days. ▶

gail carson levine

Becoming a Writer

Gail enjoyed writing the **script** for the play *Spacenapped*. She loved telling stories. One day in 1987, Gail decided to write a story. She thought that her story could become an art **appreciation** book for children. Gail wrote the book. Then she **illustrated** it with pictures of famous works of art along with some of her own drawings. She sent the book to publishers, but one publisher after another turned it down. Gail became determined to learn more about children's books. During her free time, she took a class about writing and illustrating children's books. Gail took the class mainly to learn about illustrating. However, she discovered that she loved to write.

Gail (left) studies with a college roommate. While in college, Gail had no interest in writing books.

"The Chief Royal Chambermaid heard about the pea test from the Chief Royal Window Washer. It made her curious, so she got a dried pea, because they couldn't have meant a fresh one, which would just squoosh flat. The Chief Royal Chambermaid made everything ready, just as it would be for the princess. One pea. Twenty mattresses. And a ladder."
—from p. 26 of The Princess Test (1999)

Ella Enchanted

Gail and her husband, David, are shown at their farmhouse in Brewster, New York.

For a class at The New School in New York City, Gail had to write a story. She couldn't think of a **plot**. Then she remembered the fairy tales she'd loved as a child. She wrote a story using the plot from *Cinderella*. As she began to write her story, Gail soon realized that she disliked the character Cinderella. Cinderella was a Goody Two-shoes, always doing as she was told. Gail changed the character, gave her some spirit, and named her Ella. In 1993, Gail and David moved to an old farmhouse in Brewster, New York. Gail took the train into the city to work. During the hour-and-a-half Metro-North rides, Gail wrote her own story of *Cinderella*, which became *Ella Enchanted*.

When Gail is not writing, she may be found enjoying her flower garden. ▶

Cheers

It took Gail two years to finish writing *Ella Enchanted*. She sent it and her other stories to publishers, but she received many **rejection** letters. Then in April 1996, two publishers wanted to publish *Ella Enchanted*. Gail chose the publisher HarperCollins, because they liked the story best as it was. *Ella Enchanted* was published in 1997. After working for the government for 27 years, Gail left her job. She wanted to devote her time to writing. Many people told Gail that her book might win a Newbery Award. On the day the Newbery committee made its decision, Gail came home to learn that *Ella Enchanted* had won a 1998 Newbery Honor.

Gail and another author, Robert Munsch, each ◀ received the Young Reader's Award at the Arizona Library Association Conference.

The Newbery Award and Newbery Honor Awards are the most important awards given to children's books. The award committee cheered Gail when she won the Newbery. They cheered again when she told them she was working full-time as a writer.

Giving Her Readers More

Gail's new editor had her **revise** other stories she'd written. One story was based on her father's past. During the 1920s, David Carson grew up in a Hebrew **orphanage** in **Harlem**. He wouldn't talk about his past, but Gail was curious about it. Gail's book *Dave At Night* was based on one thing her father told her. He used to sneak out to buy candy to sell to the other orphans. Gail also wrote a story based on the fairy tale "Toads and Diamonds." Gail's editor asked her to make the story longer. Her story was titled *The Fairy's Mistake*. It was the first book in a series of retold fairy tales, called The Princess Tales.

Gail says that Dave At Night is her favorite of all her books. While writing it, she learned about her family's Jewish history and about African American history and New York City's past. "I did a fair amount of research," Gail says. "I read books about the 1920s and the orphanage my father lived in. I visited museums and libraries. I conducted interviews. I visited the locations where the book takes place."

Ella Enchanted won many awards, including the American Library Association Notable Children's ▷ Book and an ALA Best Book for Young Adults.

gail carson levine

At the Farmhouse

The walls of Gail and David's 200-year-old farmhouse are covered with paintings. Many were painted by Gail, her family, and friends. Gail and David have no children, but they share their home with a new Airedale dog named Baxter. Gail works in her office upstairs. She has been writing more books for The Princess Tales series. One afternoon a week, Gail teaches creative writing to middle-school students and teenagers who like to write. She loves to see her students grow as people and as writers. She is also writing a book for children about how to write stories. Gail's book about writing is based on her years of teaching. She hopes the book will help many young writers.

◁ Gail is shown here with her dog, Jake. She and David have a new dog named Baxter.

Gail likes to visit schools and to talk with the children who read her books. One of the things Gail shares with children is her worst rejection letter from a publisher. It made her upset, but it did not stop her from writing. Gail tells children that if they never give up, they can succeed, too.

In Her Own Words

Gail is photographed with some of the students she teaches.

Why did you decide to focus on writing for children?
There was never any question. I've been a kids' book writer from the start. I think it's because my most important reading experiences were when I was a child. When I write I remember the reader I was, and that younger self is my imagined audience. If she's interested in what I'm writing, then all is well.

Which one of your characters do you most identify with, and why?
Wilma in *The Wish* is more like me than any of my other characters. I had an unpopular year [in school], as she does. Mine was tenth grade. But I also identify with Ella, because I try hard not to be too obedient.

What's a typical working day for you?
Wake up at 7:30 A.M. Eat breakfast. Go for a romp with my husband and dog. Return home and meditate. Start working late morning or early afternoon. Work till 9:00 P.M. or 10:00 P.M., with interruptions for meals. Work can also be answering fan mail, looking at contracts, preparing speeches, and the like.

What do you enjoy best about doing your job?
I enjoy just about all of it, although writing isn't always pleasurable. Sometimes a trip to the dentist is more fun. But when it goes well, writing is thrilling. I'm delighted when I come up with something completely new or when I write something funny.

If you weren't a writer, what would you be doing instead?
Sometimes I think that if I had to stop writing for some reason, I'd like to try my hand at stand-up comedy.

Glossary

appreciation (uh-pree-shee-AY-shun) Thankfulness for someone or something.

character (KAYR-ik-tur) A person or an animal that appears in a story.

commercial (kuh-MER-shul) Having to do with business or trade.

illustrated (IH-luh-strayt-ed) Created pictures that help to explain a story, poem, or book.

Jamaica (juh-MAY-kuh) An island country in the Caribbean Sea.

Harlem (HAR-lum) A community in New York City where many African American people live.

orphanage (OR-fuh-nihj) A home for children who don't have parents.

philosophy (fuh-LAH-suh-fee) The study of the nature of knowledge.

plot (PLOT) The events that happen in a story.

published (PUH-blishd) Having had a book, story, article, or poem printed so that people can read it.

rebelled (ruh-BELD) Disobeyed the people in charge.

rehearse (ree-HERS) To practice something, such as a play.

rejection (ree-JEK-shun) To be turned down or refused.

revise (ree-VYZ) To make corrections or improvements in something.

script (SKRIPT) The written story of a play, movie, radio, or television program.

unemployed (uhn-ehm-PLOYD) To be without a job.

Index

Web Sites

Due to the changing nature of Internet links, PowerKids Press has developed an online list of Web sites related to the subject of this book. This site is updated regularly. Please use this link to access the list: www.powerkidslinks.com/aa/gailclev/